Celilo Falls: Remembering Thunder

Photographs From the Collection of Wilma Roberts

Wasco County Historical Museum Press

Cover Photo: Salmon fisherman at Celilo Falls on the Columbia River. *Photo by Wilma Roberts.*

©1997 by Wasco County Historical Museum

All rights reserved. No part of this book may be reproduced in any manner without the express written consent of the publisher, except in the case of brief excerpts in critical reviews and articles. All inquiries should be addressed to the Wasco County Historical Museum, P.O. Box 998, The Dalles, Oregon 97058.

Carolyn Z. Shelton, Editor.
Design by River Graphics.

Printed in the United States of America

First Edition, 1997
10 9 8 7 6 5 4 3 2 1

International Standard Book Number: 0-9657586-1-3 (paperback)
0-9657586-0-5 (hardcover)

The Wasco County Historical Museum interprets and preserves the history of what was once the largest organized county in the United States. It is an exciting place where people can learn about their past and make their way into the future. Located at Crate's Point near The Dalles, Oregon, overlooking the magnificent Columbia River are the Wasco County Historical Museum, Columbia Gorge Discovery Center, and Oregon Trail Living History Park.

This is the first publication of the Wasco County Historical Museum Press.

*This book is dedicated with thanks to my friends
who also acknowledged this beautiful spot and whose work has contributed to this book.*
—Wilma Roberts

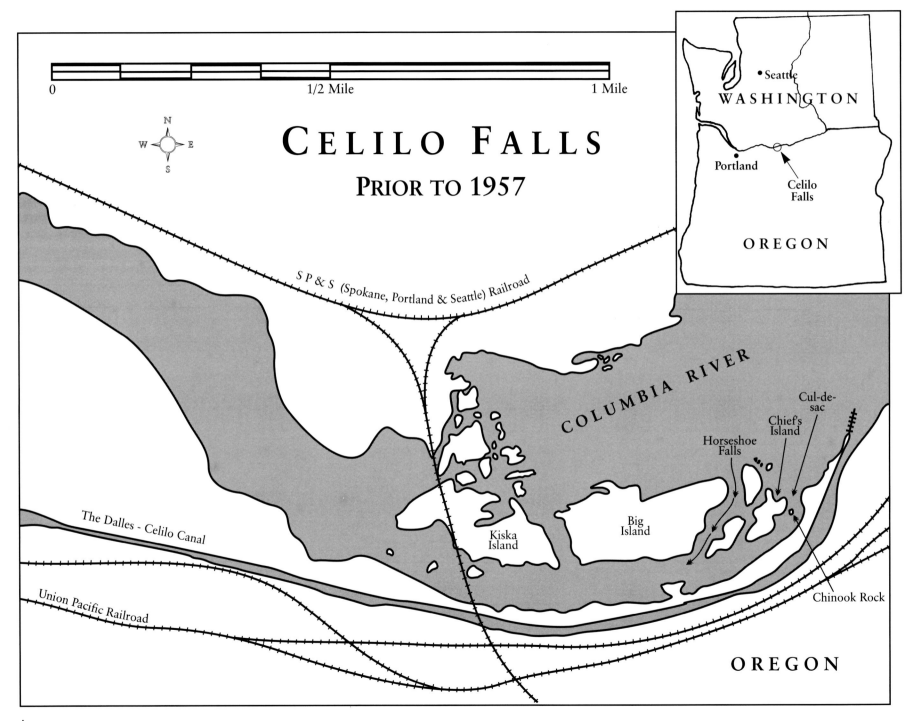

Contents

Map iv

WILMA ROBERTS: THE PHOTOGRAPHER—Mary Dodds Schlick 3

THE PLACE—Carol A. Mortland 7

WYAM: ECHO OF FALLING WATER—Elizabeth Woody 11

A FISHERMAN'S VIEW—Frederick K. Cramer 15

PHOTOGRAPHS FROM THE COLLECTION OF WILMA ROBERTS 18

Acknowledgments and Photo Credits 74

For Further Reading 75

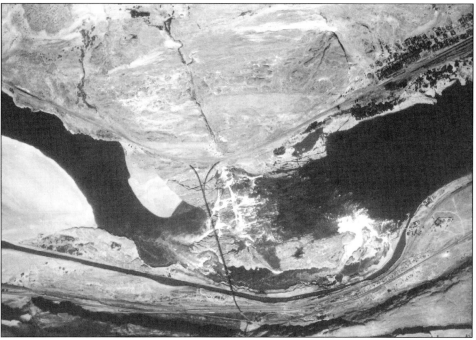

Aerial photograph of Celilo Falls area on the Columbia River.

Courtesy U.S. Army Corps of Engineers, Portland District

Wilma Roberts

Sherry Jones Photo, courtesy of Tom Jones Photography

Wilma Roberts: The Photographer

A tiny girl stood on tiptoes at the window of the train as it slipped westward along the Columbia River. She wanted to catch sight of the Indians fishing at Celilo Falls. The conductor had just passed through the train to alert passengers that they would soon reach this famous place.

The child was three-year-old Wilma McCarty on her first train ride, traveling from the family ranch near Echo to her grandparents' home at The Dalles accompanied only by two young cousins. The year was 1917.

That early glimpse foreshadowed the critical role Wilma McCarty Roberts would have in capturing on film the beauty and vitality of Celilo Falls, that ancient place where the river roared over basalt and fish beat their way against the flood toward home. For little more than a decade, from the end of World War II until the falls were drowned beneath the waters impounded behind The Dalles Dam in 1957, Roberts recorded this place. . .a place of great importance to the Native peoples of the Columbia for thousands of years.

"I was looking everywhere for photos," Roberts says of her early days as a serious photographer. "Celilo intrigued me for its uniqueness, for its ability to stop onlookers in their tracks," she recalls. "Everywhere there was a picture—fishermen standing on precarious spots, the color of the light in the afternoon through the mist, the rainbows."

The idea of a way of life going back into the Ice Age, of a people doing what their fathers had done before them for thousands of years, was fascinating to Roberts. However, documenting history was not her primary goal in taking these photographs. "I was trying to take a good photo from the standpoint of composition, an artistic presentation that would generate an emotional response in a viewer."

Although Wilma Roberts began serious study of photography as an adult, the art was not new to her. "I can't remember when I didn't take pictures," she says. "Photography was my mother's hobby; she let us use her camera." Roberts remembers playing with her mother's negatives, printing them on proof paper under glass in the sun.

Roberts' first camera came to her when she was about eight, on a trip to Pendleton. Playing miniature golf, her cousin won an Eastman Kodak box camera, she remembers. He didn't want the camera and handed it to Wilma. This was the beginning of a long series of cameras in the photographer's life.

Born in 1914, Wilma Roberts grew up on a big ranch in a valley known as Butter Creek 40 miles west of Pendleton, 11 miles from Echo. It was a real community. Roberts recalls dinners with the neighbors on Sundays and much visiting back and forth. An Indian trail crossed the ranch and she remembers the men asking her grandfather to go with them over to the river to meetings.

Graduating in a class of three from a one-room school, Wilma enrolled at Oregon State College at fifteen. She planned to major in photography, but her high school had not offered the required art or chemistry classes. She chose home economics, a course which included both subjects. In the summer, Wilma worked in a fruit packing house at The Dalles and met her future husband, Lawrence Roberts, a fellow Oregon State student. When the banks closed in 1933 during the Great Depression, Wilma had to drop out of college. She found a job in The Dalles, later marrying Roberts, who was employed by the Union Pacific Railroad.

Their son, Casey, was born in 1939. When he was six months old, her life changed in two important ways. A friend was quitting her job hand-coloring photographs at Everett Olmstead's Elite Studio. The friend suggested to Roberts that she apply. Jobs were scarce, and she had no experience. "Just fake it," the friend said. Wilma did, developing one of the skills she is known for today, that of bringing a black and white print to life with color.

At about the same time, a staphylococcus epidemic swept The Dalles. Many died. Seriously ill, Wilma asked the doctor to try sulfa, a new untested drug she had read about. The drug saved her life but left her hearing seriously impaired, speeding the effect of a hereditary condition in her family. With the same quick mind that took her to college at 15, she mastered lip-reading and continues to utilize each advance in technology that helps her communicate. "I've enjoyed a lot of life since," she says of the choice to try the drug.

Employment at Elite Studio was the beginning of Roberts' development as a photographer. Originally established in the 1890s by pioneer photographer Benjamin Gifford, the studio has played an important role in photographic history in the Northwest. It wasn't long before Wilma not only was coloring photos, but setting up a camera shop for Olmstead's son Mel when he returned from service in World War II.

Interest in photography boomed in the post-war years. "We could sell anything," she recalls. As they closed the shop on weekends, Mel O, as he was known, would hand Roberts a new camera and tell her to try it out. The photographer started shooting in color with her own Argus C3, then on to Leica and Pentax, now with Canon. Looking back at those early slides, she is flabbergasted that the images are so good.

Wilma's husband understood her passion for the art. On Sundays, they often sought out spots where she could look for pictures. On one such day, Lawrence Roberts was parked in the Gorge near Herman Creek, reading, while his wife was scouting out photo opportunities. A policeman stopped and asked, "Are you in trouble?" "Yes," Roberts replied, "I'm married to a photographer."

To learn more, Wilma Roberts studied painting and began analyzing photos in exhibitions. The photographer began to submit slides to the Photographic Society of America (PSA) salons, later serving as a national judge herself. In 1987, she was honored as a Fellow of PSA. She has contributed to other photographers' development as an active member of The Dalles Camera Club and through national seminars and those offered with her partners in Old West Ventures, Mel Olmstead and watercolorist Phil Tyler.

Wilma purchased the store's black and white negatives and all images of Old West Ventures, and continues to fill orders for photos that bring the essence of the West to homes across the country. She also offers the Old West Horse Drive held each fall near Tumalo, Oregon, where photographers are able to capture rare living scenes of early ranching days.

Through the years Wilma Roberts has traveled the world in search of the photographs that form her huge archive. Professional photographers nationwide recognize much of her work. However, the Celilo scenes are little known outside the Columbia Gorge. She has submitted only a few of these photos to salons for judging, explaining that they are so precious she has been afraid something would happen to them. Local viewers have enjoyed the photographs at her gallery and in the multi-media presentations she has developed for fund raisers for tribal communities and projects in The Dalles.

Although this book presents only a small portion of Wilma Roberts' Celilo Falls portfolio, it is something the photographer has been dreaming of for many years—an opportunity for the larger public to know and appreciate this historic place that once surged with the life and beauty captured in her photographs.

—Mary Dodds Schlick

Indian family photographed near Butter Creek, Oregon, c. 1910, by Wilma Roberts' mother.

Photograph by Laura Spencer McCarty

Mary Dodds Schlick has lived near the Columbia River or its tributaries on the Colville, Warm Springs, and Yakama reservations. Author of *Columbia River Basketry, Gift of the Ancestors, Gift of the Earth*, she now resides in the community of Mt. Hood, in Oregon's Hood River Valley.

Dark rock surfaces on the banks and cliffs along the Columbia River and its tributaries were ideal for petroglyphs and pictographs.

THE PLACE

Writing or speaking of Celilo Falls brings out the superlatives, all true. It is true that the Celilo Falls-The Dalles area, before closing The Dalles Dam gates in 1957, was the greatest Indian fishery on the Columbia River and one of the most important river fisheries in the world. It is true also that the adjacent communities of Native Americans living in the Celilo Falls-The Dalles area comprise one of the oldest continuously-inhabited communities on the North American continent.

The Columbia River, which drains much of the Pacific Northwest and northern Rocky Mountains, has been cutting its way to the Pacific Ocean for some ten million years though the greatest lava flow in North America. In the past two million years, fluctuations in climate resulted in four dramatic glacial advances south into the continental United States, each followed by a warm dry period. The last warm epoch resulted in the periodic melting of an enormous ice dam which blocked prehistoric Lake Missoula. As a result, from about 16 to 13 thousand years ago, the largest floods the world has known rushed out of western Montana, across eastern Washington, and down the Columbia River Gorge, further eroding everything in their path.

For Native Americans, Celilo has been a dominant geologic feature of the mid-Columbian area, rivaled only by the Cascades downstream. The specific characteristics of Celilo, located ten miles east of the Dalles and two hundred miles upstream from the mouth of the Columbia, were created by the crashing waters of these enormous floods.

Archaeological evidence in the form of stone blades, scrapers, and bone artifacts demonstrate that humans have lived in The Dalles-Celilo region for at least 11,500 years. However, several artifacts found during the building of The Dalles Dam suggest that humans lived in the mid-Columbian area before the catastrophic Bretz Floods occurred. Numerous salmon vertebrae are evidence that the area was already a major fishery. By 10,000 years ago, large stone spear points, choppers, knives, graving tools, grooved net sinkers, bone and antler artifacts, and the bones of rabbit, beaver, otter, muskrat, badger, and marmot indicate other subsistence activities of these early occupants. A continuous deposit of artifacts over thousands of years demonstrates the importance of this area to humans down through time, an importance that has continued to the present.

Since the Bretz Floods until the construction of The Dalles Dam, Celilo Falls was a series of basalt islands, rapids, and narrows at low water. It included Horseshoe Falls, reaching 22 feet in height. During the spring high waters, however, the Columbia River usually drowned the cliffs and islands of Celilo.

The Long Narrows, about eight miles downstream from Celilo, was the breaking point between west and east, north and south, where the constriction of the Columbia Gorge caused the Columbia River to "stand on edge," as so many writers note, as it struggled to get through the gap.

Celilo was a choke point where the "dry desert" of the east and "wet forest" of the west met, where environment, animals, plants, and people changed. Here was the most important point of contact between Indians from all directions.

From ancient times, The Dalles-Celilo area was one of the greatest trading sites on the North American continent. The Chinook-speaking Wasco and Wishram (Wishxam) and the Sahaptin-speaking Wyam, Skin, and Tenino who lived nearby were middlemen, exchanging objects from the mountains for those of the ocean and rivers, adding their own preserved salmon into the mix.

From the mouth of the Columbia River, traders brought ocean fish, other roots and berries, different in taste and quality from resources of the mid-Columbian region. Travelers from the Rocky Mountains and Great Plains brought horses, buffalo robes, feather headdresses, and pipestone. After ships arrived at the mouth of the river, Native people traded glass beads, metal tools, kettles, blankets, and other goods up the Columbia.

This trading center hosted an annual celebration, an enormous social gathering with aspects of a medieval fair. There were ceremonies, dancing, games, races, gambling, and all the other activities that occur when people living in isolated villages come together for a few weeks or months at a time of plenty.

This communal gathering evolved because of fishing. Archaeological evidence shows that people in the Celilo Falls-The Dalles area have been fishing for eleven thousand years and may have been doing so many thousands of years earlier.

Legend says that Coyote created Celilo Falls because the people had no fish and were starving. Five sisters blocked migration of the salmon by building a dam across the river. Coyote tricked the sisters into bringing him into their home by turning himself into a baby. When they went out digging for roots, Coyote dug out the dam. The people were then able to survive on the salmon swimming upstream. The rocks and islands of Celilo Falls from which Native Americans fished were the broken remnants of the sisters' dam.

Until the drowning of Celilo Falls, the river people of the twentieth century walked a middle path between the hunting, fishing, and gathering lives of their ancestors and the lives of the majority culture around them. This new lifeway centered on occupations suitable for an industrialized society and the schools that prepared them for those jobs. The river Indians and their neighbors still gathered, fished, talked, and traded their salmon. Now they gathered by car, fished with modern dipnets, talked as often in English as in the languages of their ancestors, and traded their salmon for cash. The game and the plants were largely gone, destroyed by the crops and domesticated animals of the invading settlers who had now been in residence for over a hundred years.

Now, more non-Indians gathered here, too. Celilo Falls' visibility from the highway caused thousands of tourists to stop, watch, and buy salmon. The sight was spectacular. Fishermen made their way on slippery walkways and cable cars to platforms perched over the swirling waters and under the rushing falls. In later years, tribal ordinances required the use of an "anchor" rope to prevent accidents. These turbulent waters sometimes caused fishermen to fall in and drown, slipping from their platforms caused by a misstep or from carelessness. All fishing then immediately ceased, and fishermen walked off their platforms, not to return until the next day.

Early spring fishing took on special importance from earlier times. After living on preserved food and occasional wild game during the winter, river Indians heartily welcomed the first fresh food of spring. They held a ceremony as soon as the first salmon was caught. People gathered and gave thanks for the return of this vital resource. The first salmon was then ceremoniously killed, cooked, and distributed.

Today, many of the old ways persist. The Columbia River prophet, Smohalla, admonished his river people not to abandon their ways nor to leave the Columbia River. Many river people remain faithful to their ways and the river, continuing to fish from platforms at traditional family sites. Others come to the river when the season permits, to place a gillnet or visit a relative still living at Celilo or one of the other settlements along the pacified Columbia.

These river Indians are practicing a way of life that extends back into our past thousands of years. They are heirs to the oldest occupation in the area. As they have back through time, the river people ensure the renewal of the salmon by observing a First Fish Ceremony.

Lewis and Clark, the first newcomers to see Celilo Falls, witnessed a First Fish Ceremony held by river Indians at Wishram Village near Celilo. I witnessed another such ceremony 190 years later, on April 28, 1996, not far upriver at Rock Creek Longhouse. With people of the river, I ate salmon and other traditional foods, marveling at the heritage to which we all are heir, here on the mid-Columbia.

— Carol A. Mortland

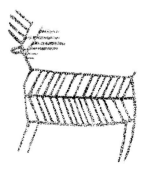

Carol A. Mortland is an anthropologist and archaeologist at The Columbia Gorge Discovery Center and Wasco County Historical Museum with degrees from Washington State University and a doctorate from the University of Oregon. She teaches prehistory of the mid-Columbian area.

Women from Celilo Village view the ancient falls prior to the death of Celilo.

Wyam: Echo of Falling Water

For more than twelve thousand years, Wyam (Celilo Falls) was an important trade center on the Chewana (Columbia River). It was part of a network that extended from California to Alaska, as far east as Missouri, and eventually west to Hawaii. The civilizations of the Northwest that preceded the advent of the Euro-Americans, Asian-Americans, Polynesian-Americans, and African Americans were sustained by an elaborate societal structure of individual cultures and sovereign governments. It has been described by the leaders at Warm Springs as a system embodied by the phrase *tee-cha-meengsh-mee sin-wit na-me ad-wa-taman-wit*. (At the time of creation the Creator placed us in this land and gave us the voice of this land and that is our law.)

These unwritten laws sustained the environment and its people to ensure the renewal of abundance, especially the seasonal return of the spawning salmon, the *nusook*. The fishing and extensive trade routes along the river and its tributaries created a cultural bounty which the newcomers, also, were welcome to share, in order to sustain themselves.

Wyam was the pivotal trade center of the Sahaptin-speaking people (Yakama, Umatilla, Walla Walla, Warm Springs, Wanapums, Wyampums, and others) and the Wasco/Chinookan-speaking people. "Great Rendezvous" would occur at Wyam, where wealth was exchanged and alliances formed. Marriages were arranged, betrothal ceremonies performed, horses traded and raced, gambling—such as stick games—was enjoyed, and families were reunited. It was also here that information was exchanged and passed along: news from across the continent, the announcement of Lewis and Clark's arrival in the Northwest, tribal news, and gossip.

For the Wyampums and Warm Springs people, Wyam was not only a trade and communication center, it was also the heart of their daily lives. Here were the most significant fisheries along the Middle Columbia River, with fishing sites passed along only through inheritance. Fishing (dip netting) was done from immense platforms built above the whitewater on fishing rocks above the falls. The first salmon of the season was honored by ceremony and a salmon feast was held to give thanks for the return of the salmon.

Salmon was a key element in the spiritual framework of my people: purity of foods, purity of thought, purity of body. It was part of the litany of praise to those things without which life wouldn't be possible (which also included the deer, the roots, the berries, the sun, the earth, and the water). The entire fish was used, except for the guts. Nothing was wasted. Packed with vitamins, beneficial oils, and minerals—fresh or dried—it was nearly complete nutritionally. Massive amounts of salmon were stored over the winter, and the excess was traded for specialty items. Abundant salmon runs ensured that anyone willing to work wouldn't starve.

Wyam—the longest continuously inhabited site of human habitation in the Northwest, possibly in the U.S.—was destroyed by the U.S. Army Corp of Engineers on March 10, 1957, when the massive steel and concrete gates of The Dalles Dam closed and choked the downstream surge of the Columbia River. Six hours later and eight miles upstream, Wyam, the age-old fisheries and falls, was under water and lost forever.

Shortly before The Dalles Dam was opened, the U.S. Army Corp of Engineers met with leaders from Yakama, Warm Springs, Umatilla, and Nez Perce, and a settlement was reached. Wyampum's chief, Tommy Thompson, who was still living at Celilo Village, refused to "signature his salmon away" and instead held a prayer and song ceremony exhorting Congress to vote against the dam's opening. Chief Thompson said, "The Almighty took a long time to make this place." An eloquent leader, who possessed a spiritual integrity like so many great leaders of the area, he was one of many who still revered the ancient lifeways given to the people by the Creator at the time of creation. He taught, by example, respect for the natural laws tribes adhered to, which ensured that no more was taken than needed and that the rest continued to grow and proliferate.

The tribes had always maintained an internal system of checks and balances for maintenance and harvest. We honored the natural laws of the earth, its physical requirements. We followed cultural and spiritual systems and worked collaboratively through an ancient, nondestructive process to promote health and prosperity for the land, families, and nonhuman beings that live here. This practice was handed down from one generation to the next, in home life, work, community, and the longhouse.

The unconscionable drowning of Wyam—Celilo Falls—marks a crucial point in our collective history. It destroyed a major cultural site and rent a multi-millenial relationship of a people to a place. After nearly four decades, Celilo Falls is still talked about and remembered as the heart of our homeland. It was like a mother, nourishing us, and is remembered as a place of great of peace.

— Elizabeth Woody

Excerpted from "Wyam: Echo of Falling Water" in *Seven Hands, Seven Hearts: Prose and Poetry* by Elizabeth Woody, © 1994 by Elizabeth Woody, published by The Eighth Mountain Press, Portland, Oregon 1994. Reprinted by permission of the author and publisher.

Elizabeth Woody is of Yakama, Warm Springs, Wasco and Navajo descent. A writer, artist, teacher, and basketmaker, Woody's second book of poems, *Luminaries of the Humble,* received the William Stafford Memorial Poetry Award from the Pacific Northwest Booksellers Association in 1995. *Seven Hands, Seven Hearts* is her third book. She lives in Portland, Oregon.

Overview of Celilo Falls, Horseshoe Falls upper right, Wishram railroad bridge at left, The Dalles-Celilo Canal along the bottom.

A Fisherman's View

Some remember the 'never silent roarings of the river.' Others say Celilo Falls was relatively quiet. Some fishermen recall the rustling, hissing sound of the water filled with air bubbles, while waiting to catch a fighting salmon in their dip nets.

Celilo Falls was the heart of the Indians' traditional fishing grounds—an ancient and historic fishing place for Native Americans. Various tribes—Yakamas, Umatillas, Nez Perce, Warm Springs, and others—were represented by scores of dipnetters, especially during the fall chinook runs from late August until late September. Large Indian fisheries existed elsewhere, but at no other place, perhaps, on the North American continent was there a native fishery so concentrated and as large within a limited area as at Celilo Falls on the Columbia River. At the peak of the fall run, Celilo was one of the greatest tourist attractions in the Pacific Northwest. Before The Dalles Dam was constructed, this majestic river was alive and ever changing, varying always in its sounds, smells, currents, eddies, strengths—enchanting and grand. Here, among the fast, swift currents and plunging waters, it was fascinating to see those large, powerful, magnificent, fighting salmon pulled from the water, sometimes two or three at a time, thrashing wildly in a dip net.

Dip nets were used at locations where salmon were forced to use eddies or restricted channels. Dip nets were hoops, often two to five feet in diameter, supporting a bag made of mesh webbing, attached to the end of a long pole. In one type, the so-called "sweep" net, the net was so arranged that the meshes would slip down on the hoop and close the opening to the net after the fish was caught. In describing this type of Indian fishing he witnessed at Willamette Falls in 1842, Captain Charles Wilkes of the United States Navy said, "The mode of using the net is peculiar: they throw it into the foam as far upstream as they can reach, and it then being quickly carried down, the fish who are running up in a contrary direction, are then caught."

In the other type of dip net, the meshes were secured to the hoop around its circumference and so did not slip or close. This "set" type was often placed in a small eddy, hugging the bank, with the net bagging out in a direction opposite to the main current, or, conversely, sometimes secured so that the net intercepted the swift current to catch fish forced into a downstream direction. Wires or ropes, attached to the hoop or pole and tied to the fishing platform or bank, helped to keep the hoop and net aligned properly in the swift water. Fish swimming in the eddy or falling back into the net were thus caught. A sharp bump on the hoop or quick jerks on the "signal string"—a piece of twine that was attached to the net itself and held in the fisherman's hand at the opposite end—was followed by pulling up the dip net as fast as possible. Hopefully, a fish was caught and the whole effort was not just a "water haul."

Spears were used at Celilo to a minor extent wherever rapids or falls caused fish to become exposed or visible in their ascent against the currents, thereby offering themselves as targets. The most effective type was the "slip-point spear." The point was mounted on the end of a pole with a cord fastened to the point at one end and secured at the other to the pole a few feet from its end. After the point, or points, was forced into the fish, it came off the pole and the salmon could then be landed with the attached short line. Sometimes, a large hook was fastened to a pole, with its line attached, and the salmon would be snagged.

The Treaty of 1855 with Indians of various Columbia River treaty tribes, among other provisions, stated "the exclusive right of taking fish in streams running through or bordering said reservations is hereby secured to said Indians, and at all other usual and accustomed stations in common with citizens of the United States. . . ." This latter category included Celilo where, in the latter part of the nineteenth and in the twentieth century, a few white men fished. I. H. Taffe once operated a small salmon cannery at Celilo, as well as some fish wheels. His operation was purchased by Seufert Bros. Company of The Dalles. Seuferts also operated the big Tumwater fish wheel on the Oregon shore there—a structure well remembered by early tourists. The Seuferts ran net seines on the seining grounds below Celilo and constructed cable crossings from the mainland to several islands to help transport fish to their fish buying stations.

I fished at Celilo for about ten days each fall from 1931 to 1937 while attending high school and college. Sometimes during those years, the fishermen received only two cents per pound for the fine salmon, sometimes only one-half cent. I remember when no money would exchange hands—only barter with the farmers—eggs, potatoes, a ham for a fish. Then beer was cheap, and Camel, Chesterfield, and Lucky Strike cigarettes were fifteen cents per pack, with Wings down to ten cents. Roll-your-own were popular, with Bull Durham and Golden Grain tobacco in tiny sacks stuffed in shirt pockets.

At 10:00 AM Sunday, March 10, 1957, the U.S. Army Corps of Engineers closed the gates at The Dalles Dam and the pool upstream began to form that drowned the Falls and fishing sites. Later that day I drove past Celilo. The fast water was gone, with a few rocks protruding yet above the nearly stilled waters. An ancient and historic fishery passed away and a great era on the Columbia—the great River-of-the-West—had come to an end. The Indians at Celilo that I saw, with their long braids and black, wide-brimmed hats, were watching solemnly as their heritage disappeared slowly under the water, bidding this revered place a silent, sad farewell.

For the loss of this fishing site, the treaty tribes, all together, were paid $27 million. This amount was the capitalized value of the average annual catch at Celilo during the five year period, 1949-1953.

— Frederick K. Cramer

Pulling a seine below Celilo Falls.

Frederick K. Cramer is the co-author with Ivan J. Donaldson of *Fishwheels of the Columbia* and author of *Recollections of a Salmon Dipnetter*. He has extensive knowledge about the history of fishing on the Columbia River.

A steam train moves eastward past Celilo Village.

W. C. "Jack" Johnson Photo

Walkway to Chinook Rock; hanging platforms on Chief's Island. Wishram railroad bridge in background.

Early Benjamin Gifford photograph of dip netter on left and spear or snag fishermen on right. Wooden fish lead that directed salmon to one of Taffe's fishwheels at upper left was destroyed by high water flows soon after it was built. Circa 1901.

The Cul-de-sac, the easiest area to reach from the road, became a favorite with photographers and a mecca for tourists.

The Cul-de-sac area, Oregon side, with Klickitat hills and town of Wishram, Washington, in background. Remnants of a Taffe fish wheel at right.

Cable car from Oregon shore at right to Chief's Island, Cul-de-sac area. The roaring sound of the river's power could be heard when approaching from the road.

Serenely taking in the scenery. Cul-de-sac area during higher flows.

Chinook Rock in foreground and hanging platforms on Chief's Island, Cul-de-sac area, taken during low water flow.

Gladys Seufert Photo

Left: "Set" type dip nets line the channel, the fishermen waiting for salmon to enter the nets. Traveling upstream in the swift currents, the salmon stayed close to the banks, seeking the easier routes afforded by small eddies.

Facing page: One salmon caught; other fishermen hoping to feel the nudge of a salmon in their net.

A fisherman patiently waits for a big one.
This photo (above) is brought to life on the facing page by Wilma Roberts' skillful hand-coloring.

Good balance and sure-footedness were essential.

Looking westward and downstream toward Horseshoe Falls. Railroad bridge in background.

Out beyond Chief's Island, hoping to catch a salmon.

Waiting, waiting and trying to stay alert.

"...the huge, roaring torrent, still rising and spreading at length, overwhelms the high jagged rock walls between them, making a tremendous display of chafing, surging, shattered currents, counter-currents, and hollow whirls that no words can be made to describe."
— *John Muir*

Riding the fish box in the Cul-de-sac area. "When he was a little lad. . .they had no cable going across to the island. They had to row across on canoes to fish."
— Flora Thompson, wife of Wyam Chief Tommy Thompson, speaking of his boyhood in *Flora's Song*.

At left, a long reach for fish, the safety rope stretched to the limit. A "sweep" dip net in action.

Right, patient fishermen at the Cul-de-Sac area.
Hand-colored by Wilma Roberts.

A long handle on this dip net. Looking eastward toward Taffe fish wheel area.

A Warm Springs family gathers with relatives and friends for one of the annual celebrations at Celilo Village.

Wild waters. Tripod on right is an anchorage for a fish box cable.

A lonely vigil among the rushing waters.

41

Left: "We have the salmon feast, very old. It signified the beginning of the first coming of the chinook salmon up the river each year. How delicious it tastes cooked this open style way!"
— Flora Thompson, in *Flora's Song*

Below: "In the fall when they spawn, then we smoke it. When we dry it, we have to keep it in a certain temperature. We do the slicing and cleaning, no pitchy wood."
— Flora Thompson, in *Flora's Song*

Pulling in a nice one.
Better than a "water haul."

Opposite: View of Cul-de-sac area hand-colored by Wilma Roberts.

At right, the plunging water of Horseshoe Falls. Wishram Bridge is in the background.

The fisherman is on his own, all by himself, on this narrow walkway to a dip net site. Chief's Island area, Klickitat Hills in background.

Cul-de-sac area. Two busy fish boxes with fishermen riding the cable. Most fish boxes were moved by engine power.

A rocky island surrounded by wild waters. Braving the slippery rocks to capture one of these thrilling views, Wilma Roberts suddenly found herself on her back, feet hanging over the water below.
Holding up her camera, she edged backward from the edge of the rock shelf, first by one elbow, then the other.

Two "set" type dip nets side by side. Which one will catch the next salmon?

Taking a rest before sweeping the waters again.

Facing page: Riding the fish box on a cable over the turbulent flow. Before the Seuferts installed the cables, fishermen reached the islands by boat.

celilo fisherman

you made your nets
and tested the knots
    seeing that they held.

little did you know
    what was to hold you
    after the sound of
    water falling
    over what
        used to be.

— Ed Edmo

Ed Edmo, a Shoshone/Bannock/Nez Perce/ Yakama poet, was a child living at Celilo when the falls disappeared. This poem has appeared in Chuck Williams' *Bridge of The Gods, Mountains of Fire* and in "These Few Words of Mine" in *Blue Cloud Quarterly,* Marvin, SD, 1984.

Horseshoe Falls area.

53

Hanging platforms, "sweep" dip nets, and fishermen. Cul-de-sac area.

Closer view of the fishermen in the center
of the photo on the facing page.
Can a fish swim the gauntlet?

55

A long reach with dip nets; fishermen anchored by safety ropes.

Plunging flows in the Cul-de-sac. Downe's Channel in foreground.

57

Reaching for a big one. Waterproof clothing was needed here, as well as the safety rope required by tribal ordinance.

Fisherman ready to push his "set" dip net into the churning water.

Tourists galore. Cul-de-sac area

Facing page: Photograph hand-colored by Wilma Roberts. Sadie Schoolie Brown of Warm Springs at Celilo with an elder relative of the family, and her children, Curtis, Charlotte (now Charlotte Shike), and, on the cradleboard, Neda (now Neda Wesley).

Every spot was fair game for fishing, no matter how precarious, even hanging platforms.

A big salmon in the net at the Cul-de-sac. Nets were kept in constant repair to prevent loss of such a catch.

Lafie Foster Photo

Tourists and more tourists. Webb Petersen riding in fishbox on left.

Facing page: Cables cross over Chinook Rock, at left of photo, to Chief's Island during low water.

Sweep dip nets in action. "The immense waters of the Columbia are one mass of foam, and force their headlong course with a frightful impetuosity..."
— Ross Cox, July, 1812.

Cul-de-sac area. Visitors, foreground, watch the use of "set" type dip nets. At the peak of the fall fishing season, Celilo Falls was probably the greatest tourist attraction in the Pacific Northwest.

"The best dip net sites are narrow, rocky cliffs, and islands, where the fish are close to shore."

— Edward Sapir, 1909

Lafie Foster Photo

Gladys Seufert Photo

Indian with dugout canoe. Circa 1900.

"After the first fish was sent by the Almighty, they had a certain day when they had a great big gathering for the salmon feast. All would play the stick game. It is an old game from time memorial."
— Flora Thompson,
Flora's Song

The day the U.S. Army Corps of Engineers released doves from Celilo Village to mark the beginning of The Dalles Dam Project, 1955. Flora Thompson is seventh from left; Wyam Chief Tommy Thompson is next to her.

Chief Thompson had said, "I am not giving up my fishing. That's all the livelihood we have."
— from *Flora's Song*

Looking downstream on the Columbia River at The Dalles Dam.

Facing page: The Dalles Dam, Oregon fish ladder in foreground.

Acknowledgements

This book is a celebration of the Grand Opening of the Wasco County Historical Museum on May 24, 1997. It is a collaborative effort of labor and love, and the culmination of Wilma Roberts' dream to see her beautiful photographs in print for all to share. Thank you to the many people who contributed financial support to this project.

The editor wishes to thank Frederick K. Cramer, Dr. Carol A. Mortland, and Mary Dodds Schlick for their dedication and many hours of work toward producing this book. It has been an honor to work with Wilma Roberts. She is an inspiration to all—a talented and vivacious photographer *par excellence*.

Photo Credits

Unless otherwise noted, all photographs were taken by Wilma Roberts.

The Other Photographers:

Gladys Seufert and her late husband, Francis, graciously allowed The Dalles Camera Shop to use all of the negatives in their family collection for resale as black and white and hand-colored photographs through the years. An excellent photographer as well as developer and printer, Gladys Seufert has made over 5,000 photos recording historic monuments in the state for the Oregon Historical Society.

Lafie Foster of The Dalles began his photography work in the late 1940s working in Mel O's Camera Shop darkroom in The Dalles. His natural talent led him to become a five-star exhibitor with the Photographic Society of America within a few years.

W. C. "Jack" Johnston of Wishram, Washington, developed an intense interest in photography about 1948. With the finest camera equipment and best techniques, he documented railroad and Celilo Falls scenery until 1957. Johnston's work appears through the courtesy of his son, Ted Newman.

Laura Spencer McCarty, the mother of Wilma Roberts, lived on the Columbia River at the mouth of the Deschutes River as a child. She attended Locust Grove School and moved to eastern Oregon after her marriage. A photographer, Laura McCarty encouraged her daughter's interest in the field. The photo on page 5 was taken near the McCarty family ranch at Butter Creek.

John Shearer, a pilot, has an orchard and wheat spray service in The Dalles. His aerial photograph appears on page 14.

J. W. Thompson of Seattle, Washington, produced many sets of slides for use in classrooms, including two on the Indians of Washington State. The photo on page 10 is from "The Indians of Eastern Washington" and is used with permission from his daughter, Lucile Munz.

Benjamin Gifford is considered one of the Northwest's great pioneer photographers. He established a commercial studio in The Dalles in the early 1890s for the purpose of making studies of the native peoples of the Columbia River. His studio later became the Elite Studio, where Wilma Roberts began producing her own photographic legacy.

For Further Reading

Allen, J. E. and M. Burns. *Cataclysms on the Columbia.* Portland, OR: Timber Press, 1986.

Boyd, Robert. *People of The Dalles, the Indians of Wascopam Mission.* Lincoln, NE: University of Nebraska Press, 1996.

Cramer, Frederick K. *Recollections of a Salmon Dipnetter.* Portland, OR: Oregon Historical Quarterly, September, 1974.

Cressman, Luther S. *Prehistory of the Far West: Homes of Vanished Peoples.* Salt Lake City, UT: University of Utah Press, 1977.

Donaldson, Ivan J. and Frederick K. Cramer. *Fishwheels of the Columbia.* Portland, OR: Binfords & Mort, 1971.

Hines, Donald M. *Celilo Tales: Wasco Myths, Legends, Tales of Magic and the Marvelous.* Issaquah, WA: Great Eagle Publishing, 1996.

Hunn, Eugene S. with James Selam and family. *Nch' i-Wana, "The Big River," Mid-Columbia Indians and Their Land.* Seattle, WA: University of Washington Press, 1990.

McKeown, Martha Ferguson. *Linda's Indian Home.* Portland, OR: Binfords & Mort, 1956.

McKeown, Martha Ferguson. *Welcome to Our Salmon Feast.* Portland, OR: Binfords & Mort, 1959.

Schlick, Mary Dodds. *Columbia River Basketry, Gift of the Ancestors, Gift of the Earth.* Seattle, WA: University of Washington Press, 1994.

Seufert, Frances A. *Wheels of Fortune.* Portland, OR: Oregon Historical Society, 1980.

Wagenblast, Joan Arrivee and Jeanne Hillis. *Flora's Song, A Remembrance of Chief Tommy Kuni Thompson of the Wyams.* 1112 Dry Hollow Road, The Dalles, OR, 97058, 1993.

Williams, Chuck. *Bridge of the Gods, Mountains of Fire: A Return to the Columbia Gorge.* New York, NY: Friends of the Earth, 1980.